ZOE PENCARROW
and THE
GOLDEN
CAGE

By
Dan Robertson

DEDICATION

"Let the little children come to me,
and do not hinder them, for the Kingdom of God
belongs to such as these."
Mark 10:14 b

"Place me like a seal over your heart, like a seal
on your arm; for love is as strong as death, its
jealousy unyielding as the grave. It burns like
blazing fire, like a mighty flame."
Song of Songs 8: 6

My God—you are unyielding, unquenchable, and eternal. Your love never ceases to amaze me. You reach into the darkest depths and bring forth your truth and life. You are abundance personified and so, so kind...You light up this world with a smile and cloak the storm clouds with your grace. Your footsteps are filled with pools and your eyes with fire. You are my best friend. Thank you!

"Those who are wise will shine like the brightness
of the heavens, and those who lead many to
righteousness, like the stars for ever and ever."
Daniel 12: 3

To my beloved, beautiful, beautiful bride. You shine with the brilliance of the One who is consuming fire, and light up my life with your love and laughter. Sometimes a river starts as a trickle in the mountains, or a spring as a bubbling pool in the desert—you are a garden fountain! You know the Source and give Him away unconditionally. You have found the *"wild parrots"* and share them with me. What an Adventure you are!

"A voice of one calling: In the desert prepare the
way of the Lord; make straight in the wilderness
a highway for our God."
Isaiah 40: 3

To Linda. Occasionally a champion arises who is not like the others. One who serves unconditionally to promote others above herself, and is prepared to make straight in the wilderness a highway for our God. Your fiery passion is a testimony of a life laid down. You truly are the Master Potter's friend and dwell in His house.

"Be strong and courageous, because you will lead
these people to inherit the land I swore to their
forefathers to give them."
Joshua 1: 6

To Debbi. Braveheart! You are not afraid to be a pioneer and sail into uncharted waters. You see things differently because you see with heaven's eyes. Your heart is moved by heaven! Your creativity is a powerful gift with all its diversity and complexities and in your hands there is great healing. You lead the lame, the blind and the weak to drink from the water of life.

"My heart is stirred by a noble theme as I recite my
verses for the king; my tongue is the pen
of a skilful writer."
Psalm 45: 1

To Iona. You have the heart of a lioness. Your boldness, courage and compassion will move the mountains and your truth and love will melt the hardest of hearts. Your words—spoken and written, will touch and change the generations. You are a Last Days champion, a quill in the hand of your Beloved.

WHAT CHILDREN ARE SAYING ABOUT

Zoe Pencarrow and The Golden Cage

Wow! This is an amazing book and I'm so glad I was one of the ones chosen to read this for the first time! I really enjoyed reading it and wanted to find out what happened next. It's just such an incredible book and it made me want to dive deeper and find out more about our great God! It made me really want to meet Jesus like she did.

Bethany, 11 years old, Wales

Amazing! I was gripped by the detailed and awesome description of Zoe's voyage through the secret world.... The characters and images in the book are so easy to imagine. It's as though one were really in the middle of the story, seeing everything with Zoe's eyes – the Eagle, the Starfish, and so much more....When Zoe falls into the rockpool, you have the feeling you're right in the rockpool with her!"

Delilah, 16 years old, Germany

CONTENTS

Chapter 1

AT THE BEACH

S ummertime. Wow! Finally, two weeks of vacation. The long dreary days of winter and the changeable spring were over at last. Beach time had begun: eating ice-creams and toasting marshmallows on roaring campfires at night. *This* was the stuff that Zoe had been waiting for. She hummed a little tune as she gathered up treasures from the rock pools, popping them into her yellow bucket to take home and add to her ever-increasing shell collection. The fresh salt air blew on her face and the waves crashed onto the beach. Zoe was thirteen — definitely grownup enough to ask her parents to go surfing, like her older brother Sam. She was, after all, a very good swimmer. The thought of riding those big waves made her heart sing. She knew she was made for adventure, even when the waves were just a little bit scary.

Sam, as usual, was acting like a horrid big brother. He had already hidden Zoe's bucket and spade earlier in the day. Now he stomped around in the rock pools each time his sister was about to pick up a beautiful shell. Zoe was growing rather tired of this game. She was wondering how she could get rid of him when she noticed something glistening near her toes. Peering down, she somehow managed to "shush" her brother.

The most unusual starfish she had ever seen was looking up at her. It was bright orange like a sunset, with golden spots that sparkled like drops of dew on a sunny spring morning. However it wasn't just its beauty that captured her attention. The arms of the starfish were moving as well, almost waving at her. Zoe gasped. *Could this be real? Was it really waving?* Just then, Sam let rip a loud "yahoo" and jumped into the rock pool with an almighty crash. Zoe instinctively closed her eyes so she wouldn't get saltwater in them.

Bother, I'm all wet. I must have fallen into the rock pool, Zoe thought, as she struggled to get her head out of the water. It was only then that she realized that she was standing up. *The rock pool couldn't possibly be this deep.* She pushed her feet down into the sand to propel herself up to the surface. Whoosh! She shot up like a rocket. Zoe held her breath as she had learned in swim class at school, and kicked her way up towards the surface. *How is this possible?* The further up she swam, the more water there seemed to be. She was surrounded by countless forms of sea life. Fish in a rainbow of colors, sea sponges, and vibrant tropical corals all waved at her as she passed by.

Zoe knew that she couldn't possibly still be in the rock pool. There was just too much water. A vast stingray glided past and hovered, as if studying her, before disappearing to the sea bed down below. Giant jellyfish in yellows and pinks puffed themselves up like hot air balloons before filling the water with streams of bubbles. When the bubbles touched other sea creatures they started to laugh and chase each other around in a game of tag. *This is bizarre,* thought Zoe; *fish don't laugh!*

The underwater world looked like a high definition 3D cartoon with its bright colors and amazing sea life. Zoe had only just arrived, but she felt like she belonged here too. Only this was not a cartoon, or a make believe world created by a clever animator or a computer program. This was for real. She could see for miles in the crystal clear water. *I had better get to the surface soon*, she thought, *before I run out of air*. But she was already taking in large gulps of water and breathing, as though it were quite normal. *Have I become a fish?* she wondered. "No you haven't," said a voice just off to her left. Zoe spun around and saw a huge starfish about the size of a car. It was beckoning her to follow. "Why, you're the same starfish I saw in the rock pool," she exclaimed, "only much bigger!" The starfish continued to wave at her until she followed. Then it gently glided down to the bottom of the seabed, stood up on two its legs and spoke; "Over there — that's where you need to go," as it pointed with one of its other legs (or were they arms?) at a giant glistening white oyster shell.

The oyster shell reminded Zoe of something that she had seen before. It was larger than life — about the size of a small house—and was covered in ridges and bumps. She peered at it as a multitude of images flickered across its surface. Thousands upon thousands of TV screens covered it, like barnacles on a boat. The nearest screen showed a young Afro-American boy crying, huddled on his bed. His clothing was dirty and his legs and arms were bruised. Behind the boy were tall buildings. *It must be somewhere in New York*, she thought.

Zoe gasped. This wasn't a movie but something that was actually happening. She was so surprised that she looked away. Her gaze fell upon another TV screen. She saw a richly dressed Arab man wearing a green turban. He looked like an oil merchant in the Middle East. Several other similarly dressed men surrounded him. The man's face was engraved with lines from years of worry. He clutched his chest and his face grimaced, as pain shot through his heart.

"This is terrible," Zoe shouted. "Someone help him, please!" Zoe could feel the comforting grip of someone holding her hand. She spun around. It was the starfish. His voice... it reminded her of someone she knew... and then she remembered. He sounded like her friend the eagle, whom she had met in an adventure long ago.

"Our God sees and hears the pain and struggles of everyone he has created. He is certainly not distant or uncaring. Instead, he longs for everyone to find him and live in his peace and freedom. God offers his unconditional love to everyone."

Zoe looked up into the starfish's eyes. They were the same intense piercing blue color as those of her old friend, the eagle... only, well, these eyes were the bluest of blues; like the depths of the sea. The starfish was smiling at her. He then looked towards the oyster shell. The oyster had opened. Light streamed out through the opening and made the shell look whiter than white. The light was warm and inviting and beckoned her to climb inside and discover more. With a leap of faith she let go of the starfish's hand and stepped into the oyster.

Chapter 2

THE HOUSE WITH
THE DAISIES

The oyster was totally different up close. It now looked like a two storey house with a large green paneled wooden door. The neat curtains in the four windows, the chimney and the red roses growing in terracotta planters on either side of the door were all strangely familiar. Zoe opened the door and found herself inside a long hallway. An umbrella stand contained neatly folded umbrellas in jellybean colors. On the other side of the hallway were hooks in the shape of daisies for hanging coats and hats. Directly in front of her an ornately carved wooden staircase curved gracefully up to the floor above. Overhead a grand chandelier sparkled. It looked like it had been made from the most exquisite crystals for a chateau somewhere in France. A fine Persian carpet lined the stairs, which ended in warm colored marble tiles with pretty daisy patterns. At any moment Zoe half expected to see a beautiful princess come gliding down the staircase, only to be swept up into the arms of her adoring prince.

The daisy pattern was everywhere. She could see it on the red velvet drapes with the golden cords and the checkered table cloths in what must have been the dining room. What was it about this house though that seemed so vaguely familiar to her? Directly in front of Zoe hung a huge painting. It wasn't the intricately carved golden frame that drew her attention but the people in it. Staring back at her was her family—mom and dad, Sam and herself! Everybody looked wiser and older than in real life. Each person was dressed in rich and elaborate clothing. Her dad was in a kind of general's uniform with gold epaulettes on his shoulders and a red sash across his chest. Mom had on an amazing sky blue ball gown and a tiara on her head. Sam appeared to be wearing what at first looked like a combat uniform. Upon closer inspection it was more like a special military uniform. Zoe was wearing a beautiful silver dress that reached down to her ankles. Where had she seen this dress before? Then she remembered. This was the same dress that she had been given in the cave of crystals in her last adventure.

Now she remembered where she had seen this house before. This was _her_ doll's house! Her daddy had bought it for her when she was just a wee button for her fourth birthday... only this one was a much much bigger one! Zoe ran through the open French doors and burst into the living room. It was just like in her doll's house! It had tartan cushions, and fine china tea cups on the table, all ready to entertain imaginary guests. Across from the table was the polished oak dresser. In the corner, the old grandfather clock was reliably ticking away. At any moment she half expected the side of the doll's house to open up and two huge eyes to peer in to rearrange the furniture and pour a cup of tea!

Just then, the grandfather clock chimed, signaling the change of the hour. In strode her old friend the eagle. She rushed up and kissed and hugged him, giggling and laughing at the same time.

"Oh, it's so good to see you again after all this time."

"I've missed you too," replied the eagle, as he put his wing lovingly around her shoulders and looked at her with his clear blue eyes. "But I had to go away for a while to swap stories with the others."

Zoe looked expectantly at the eagle, for she had learned that when the eagle turned up she was in for a wild time. The eagle was delighted to see his old friend again too. But instead of rushing off with her on a new adventure, he simply sat down next to her on the sumptuous couch. He carefully poured a cup of tea from the silver teapot on the side table next to the couch and handed it to her. The piping hot tea had the faintest hint of cinnamon and apple flavor and was so refreshing. Zoe munched away on the amazingly delicious caramel and walnut cookies. The eagle wanted to know everything that had happened since he had seen her last. He seemed to know a little of what she had been up to, but there were many details he knew nothing about. He was most interested to hear about the gifts she had been given; the fishing rod, the lures and the blue pocket knife. But most of all, the eagle wanted Zoe to talk about her time with Jesus.

Zoe said that in heaven everything was so much easier than back on earth. Since her last adventure with the eagle, Zoe really had to remember to consciously listen to Jesus every day. There were so many things to do that made it hard to have time with Jesus. She really had to make a special time each day to be quiet, and to remember to listen to him while she did things throughout the day. Zoe also explained that she had started using the fishing rod, but wasn't very good at it yet. She shyly admitted that she had even started dancing; just her and Jesus. She would go into her room to be with him, and could sometimes hear angel choirs singing while she danced. She would close her eyes (so that no one could see her!) and start dancing. Zoe could feel the glorious presence of Jesus come into her room like a warm summer's breeze. Around and around they would dance together.

Sometimes it was sort of like a waltz, and others times more like a wild war dance. They would stomp and jump, shout and clap all around her bedroom. She wondered how her parents never seemed to hear the noise! But she always had so much fun and Zoe loved being with him. Other times he would come and she would just be still and listen, as he told her secrets and shared his heart with her. On occasion, they said nothing to each other but just enjoyed each other's company as words were not even necessary. Those times were the best!

The eagle was delighted. He finished his remaining tea, and with a big beaky smile, placed the teacup back on its saucer and said, "Well done, my brave and faithful princess. You certainly have grown up and learned the most important lesson since I saw you last, time with the Lord."

Before Zoe could reply the eagle stood up and walked out of the room, indicating with his wing that she should follow him.

Chapter 3

THE CONSERVATORY AND THE GOLDEN CAGE

T hey entered a room that wasn't like anything Zoe could remember having in her doll's house.

"It's called a conservatory," explained the eagle, as if he were reading her thoughts. "Our Father has prepared many rooms for each of us to explore. As we overcome the challenges in each room he allows us to discover the next one. The rooms all contain heavenly treasures. We can choose to stay in any one of them, or continue to explore new rooms, when it's time."

"How many rooms are there in my house, and how do I know when it's time to move on to the next one?"

"Only the Father knows that answer. He will tell you each time you are ready for the next room. My job is to help you discover the treasures in each room and use them wisely. Only you can decide when it's time to move to the next room. I can prompt and guide you, and offer you my counsel. But you must be responsible for the choices you make. It's all part of the Father's plan, how he helps us grow up and become more like him."

"You must be very old and wise to know all of these things. I wonder if I will ever be old or wise enough to know everything that I need to know," Zoe pondered. "My dad has lots of gray hair and my mom says he still makes silly mistakes."

The eagle smiled. "We are all still learning and we all still make mistakes. But because we are God's children he loves us dearly. He can deal with our messes when we muck things up, and he always gives us his wisdom and counsel to make right choices. I will show you one of the ways you can learn this."

Zoe thought that maybe the eagle was about to show her a very large book crammed full of important stuff that she could learn. She had even heard of people doing yoga and meditation to try and gain more knowledge and wisdom. She hadn't quite figured out how it was supposed to work though. Surely to be cleverer you needed to be filled up with much more "cleverness," not try and empty yourself of whatever you already had! Besides, from what she had already experienced from God's way of doing things, it was more about trust and obedience. God had a lovely way of filling a person up with his presence, sort of like a car going to the gas station and being filled up with gas.

The eagle led Zoe to another room. The annex was a strange place. Its walls were painted a rich vibrant green that stretched up to the ceiling, three stories high. One of the walls was made completely of glass and gave off a warm, milky green glow. Sunlight streamed in through the wall of glass and danced on the floor. The room was full of plants, but completely bare of furniture, apart from a rusted wrought iron table that stood in the middle of the room.

I wonder why the table is all rusted and neglected, she thought, *as everything else in this amazing house is so beautiful.* But it wasn't just the old table that caught Zoe's attention. Two green parrots sat in a golden cage on the table.

They were huddled together and didn't appear to be moving. At first Zoe thought that the birds were dead. But then she could see a slight movement of their bodies as they breathed in and out. Their eyes were partly closed as though they were asleep. She inched towards them. Suddenly their eyes shot open. Vivid grass green eyes studied the girl and the eagle as they approached.

"Why are the parrots so sad?" Zoe asked.

"What do you think?"

She thought about their recent conversation and the eagle's promise that God would show her more of his wisdom and counsel. As she thought about this she noticed a tiny movement on a nearby potted plant. Zoe peered down and saw a tiny praying mantis. "Wow," she said, "that's the answer! Prayer! It's about talking with Jesus and listening to what he says. Jesus, why are the parrots so sad, and what can we do to help them?"

Peace descended on her thoughts like a snuggly blanket. In her mind she saw a scene of thousands of parrots, just like the ones in the cage, but flying free. They were calling and singing and playing as they flew. The sound of their wings filled the air like the rush of a mighty river. Zoe knew the meaning of the vision. The two caged birds were meant to fly free with the rest of the flock of wild parrots.

"What should I do?" Zoe whispered. Hearing and seeing nothing more, she opened her eyes.

Next to the cage she spotted a strange flower growing in a pot, which she hadn't seen before. The flower was dark red and had the most amazing perfume. It smelled sort of sweet, but wild and tangy all at once. The flower petals radiated out like a fan or a wheel and inside them were lots of crinkly pink stamens. The stamens reminded her of her own wavy hair that went especially crinkly just after it had been washed. There were three prongs near the middle of the flower that looked like nails. In the very center was a tiny white object. Zoe looked at the eagle and then back at the beautiful flower.

"It's a passionflower," said the eagle.

Just then, a very large plump bumblebee flew in to the flower and buzzed around happily collecting the abundant pollen, before clambering out and flying off.

"Keep looking and asking," encouraged the eagle.

Zoe listened, looked and felt Jesus saying to touch the center of the flower. She reached out and something broke off in her fingers. She instantly pulled her hand back. The object she was holding was very smooth and white, and shone like the moon.

"It's beautiful," she said. "What is it?"

"It's a pearl."

"What does this mean?"

"You are a very curious little girl," said the eagle smiling, "but that's how the Lord has made you. To become all that he has meant you to be, you need to fear, love and trust God more than yourself. If you search for him as the most precious hidden treasure, you will find him. He is like this pearl. As you seek him out, he will always be there for you. He will reveal his beauty and give you all the wisdom and knowledge you need. You will become more like him. Just like this pearl, God will cover you with his presence and make you strong, so you can shine in difficult situations. When you first saw the passionflower, you knew it was a flower but didn't know what kind. But when you ask Jesus for understanding he will always tell you what you need. Sometimes he answers straight away. Other times, he seems to take ages to answer and even asks us questions. But he always hears, listens and answers—even if the answer is not exactly as we imagined! We are his beloved children and he loves it when we talk with him."

Zoe held up the pearl and slowly turned it around in her fingers. It was smooth and sparkled in the light. She knew what she must do. She turned to the eagle and said, "These parrots were not meant to be in cages. They are supposed to fly with the rest of the flock and be free."

The eagle smiled and nodded. Zoe walked over to the cage and opened the door. The parrots hopped out onto her wrist, let out a squawk of delight and flew out the nearest window. They were gone.

Chapter 4

THE FEAR OF THE LORD

The conservatory seemed rather empty without the parrots. Although there were many plants growing in the room, it no longer seemed complete any more. The eagle looked at Zoe and said, "The room hasn't really changed but you have. You have outgrown this doll's house and now it's time to leave."

"Where are we going?" asked Zoe.

"To follow the parrots," replied the eagle.

The eagle led Zoe through a door into a sunny bedroom. Neatly folded on the bed was an amazing jacket. It was made of material that was the same green color as the conservatory wall. Yet when she held it up against herself to try it for size it shimmered and appeared to change color. The color was transformed into vibrant reds, turquoises, and vivid yellows, depending on how the light caught the material. Zoe put the jacket on. It reached down to her knees, and she spun around in front of the large free standing antique mirror. Inside of the coat were stitched many pockets where you could store all sorts of secret things and treasures like feathers and sea shells. The jacket was lined in silver and gold and reminded Zoe of the armor that she had worn in her last adventure.

She wondered what to do next. She was feeling not quite properly dressed when the eagle indicated that she should go over to an old sea chest and open it. Zoe's face lit up as she opened the lid. There was her sword. It felt so good to have her old friend back again. She started digging deeper in the chest, looking for her belt to attach the sword to her waist. But the eagle gently pulled her back.

"Jesus seldom does things the same way twice. You have used this sword many times before. Now you are no longer to wear the sword around your waist. You must become the sword."

"What do you mean?" Zoe asked, feeling rather confused.

"Now that you are wearing the coat of the "Fear of the Lord," you can no longer just say and do anything you want. You must learn to only speak what you hear Father God saying, and do what he shows you. Remember, your words are powerful and can bring great blessing or curse, life or death."

Zoe was still puzzled by what the eagle was saying.

"You must eat the sword," said the eagle.

Zoe's eyes became as large as dinner plates.

"Eat the sword?" she exclaimed. "I'll be cut to pieces! I'm not one of those people at the circus!"

The eagle waited patiently until Zoe had calmed down, and then took her by the hand.

"Jesus shows and teaches many things. But he doesn't just want to come and then leave again. He wants to be involved with every part of your life—to live in every room in your house and then go off on great adventures together."

Zoe nodded.

"You can control how much space and how many rooms in your house Jesus can have. People let Jesus visit them at the front door when they need him. But they never let him in, and just slam the door in his face, once he answers their prayers. Some people invite him into the sitting room for a once a week Bible study or home group. Then they can go about the rest of their week without letting him ever see the other rooms of their house. If we really want to love and know him it's all about total access, and no limits. He's not bothered by a messy house or what's stashed away in the closet. Actually he came to do the house renovations and a makeover! And it's free. The rooms of your house are the places in your heart. You've already said you want him in every area of your life. Remember the bridal dress he gave you last time you were here, and the wonderful dance that you had together?"

Zoe thought back to the exhilarating dance she had had with Jesus in her new bridal dress. She felt so loved and special—his very own princess.

"Jesus sees you as his bride every day. But you can shut the door of your heart in his face at any time." The eagle looked sad.

"Alright, if Jesus wants me to eat the sword I'll do it. I understand now that's what he wants me to do."

Without further ado, Zoe reached out, picked up the sword and plunged it into her mouth.

Chapter 5

CONSUMED BY HIS FIRE

There was a sharp pain as the sword slid into Zoe's mouth. She felt like she was being cut in half. Pain that burned like fire swept through her whole body. She could feel every part of her being coming under the microscope of God. He could see everything; all her pain and joy, good and bad decisions—nothing was hidden from the all-seeing eyes of the Lord. Zoe wanted to scream and run away because she felt so ashamed. But she knew that there was nowhere to hide, nowhere she could escape, to go beyond his presence. He was everywhere.

The sword continued to penetrate deeper into her being. She felt wave after wave of compassion and grace washing over and covering her mistakes. As each bad memory was brought into his light, God's grace covered it up like a huge red blanket until it was no longer visible. She could actually see the blood of Jesus covering her sins beneath this blanket of grace. Jesus took the bad and painful memories out of her and into his own body, as he hung on the cross. How could anyone possibly stand in his presence who had not been covered and washed clean by his precious blood? He was so clean, so holy. Now, she too was clean and whole again. She felt light as a feather. She looked at Jesus' face that shone before her. It was the face of pure joy and radiant beauty, looking adoringly at his precious Bride.

Zoe looked around. She was no longer in the bedroom but standing on the rim of a gigantic disc or was it a sphere... she couldn't tell. The air was charged with electricity and tinged with an emerald green color. It pulsated with life. Lightning flashed around her. Radiant beings she could not begin to describe circled around her. They darted back and forth with tremendous speed to and fro from the center of the awesome green light. Each creature appeared to have six wings but they moved so fast their bodies and wings were a blur. They cried out, "Holy, Holy, Holy is the Lord Almighty."[1] When they spoke, it was like a thunder clap sounding and everything shook.

Zoe could no longer stand. Her legs buckled and she fell down flat on her face. The crescendo of voices, fire and the thick heavy presence of the Lord increased. It was like being inside the middle of a volcano as it was exploding, and a mega earthquake, all mixed together. The pressure was immense. Miraculously, her life was not squeezed out of her. Feathers and wings brushed her face as strong hands pulled her up to her feet, holding her tightly. Without this support, she would have crumpled like paper in a furnace. On either side of her stood two immense beings. Fire encircled their bodies and yet she was not consumed by it. She couldn't make out their faces, as each was blurred by the movement of their massive wings. Their bodies were covered with something that looked like interlocking gold-plated armor, resembling fish scales and bird feathers. Around their waists they wore golden belts, and blue sashes covered their chests. The presence of the Lord saturated their being. Zoe would have collapsed again if they had not continued to hold her up. One of the immense beings turned and for a brief moment Zoe caught a glimpse of the creatures' eyes through the blurring wings. They were piercing like radiant fire, and glowed like the hottest furnace. These were the kind of eyes that could look into the deepest darkest places and see everything—there was no escaping their burning gaze!

Zoe wanted to turn and flee. The eyes were so awesome, so terrifying. But she froze. Within those burning, piercing eyes she saw a passionflower—the same one she had seen in the conservatory. These eyes were the eyes of love. These eyes were filled with love because they had been looking, gazing, and feasting upon the One who was the author and source of all love—the Lord. She was captivated by the eyes of these creatures. They contained mysteries and galaxies and the secret wisdom of God. These eyes had seen plans and promises and unfulfilled great destinies. The eyes stared at her. Their piercing gaze held her, watching her every movement, penetrating her very being. They did not blink, they did not move. She thought that she was going to die or explode like a supernova. But she couldn't look away.

"Do you want what the Father wants?" asked one of the Seraphim (she later read in her Bible that's what they were).

"Yes," stammered Zoe, not exactly sure of what she was agreeing to.

One of the Seraphim studied her face for a moment before letting her go. While the other one still held her firmly the Seraph flew over to the source of light. The glowing mass surrounded him as he threw himself on the ground, worshipping the Lord. The cloud of glory rolled over the Seraph, covering him from her view.

Zoe did not know how long she stood there. It could have been minutes, it could have been hours. In this place, time was not measured as it was on earth. Zoe was just about to ask the Seraph who was holding her up if they should do something, when the glory cloud opened up. Out walked the other Seraph. The flames weren't just burning on his body now. They had intensified and were burning within him as well. Zoe could see into his body and see the raging fire within him. He was whiter than white light. His whole being was consumed by the intense white flame of the Lord.

The radiance of this heavenly being was awesome. But the light that came from the glory cloud was brighter still. *The Lord must be in the center of the glory cloud*, she thought.

The Seraph strode out to her. He stretched out his hand and touched Zoe's head. Radiant beams of pulsating light filled her body. Her body rippled and vibrated as energy pulsated through her. All the atoms and subatomic particles down to the single, minutest part of her existence were realigned into the divine plan and purpose of God. Zoe felt taller and stronger than ever before and more desperate and dependent on him. She knew that she was so loved and cherished by this wonderful, awesome God. She knew in her innermost being that she belonged to him, and was his forever.

Chapter 6

I GIVE YOU THE MORNING STAR

The fire continued to surge through Zoe's body. Then, without warning, it stopped. The Seraph let go of her and amazingly, she was able to stand without his support. A gentle wind began to blow from within the glowing cloud of glory. Zoe was transfixed by the fiery cloud. Voluminous plumes of smoke and fire billowed up like a tent blowing in the wind, as the cloud danced before her. The wind got stronger. The clouds of smoke began to unfold from its center like large double doors made from sail cloth. The wind subsided and the most wonderful aroma filled the air. It was almost indescribable. It sort of smelled like fields in the summer time; strawberries, roses, lavender, lilies and jasmine flowers all mixed up together. The fragrance was so intoxicating that Zoe thought that she was going to fall over again. She felt the incredible joy and love for her that radiated out from the center of the cloud. The waves of joy were like ripples when a stone is thrown into water. It was like spring and summer time all rolled into one. Zoe wanted to dance, and sing, and roll around and around on the ground and laugh, and jump as high as she could into the sky and touch the stars... Suddenly out of the well of love and eternal source of goodness, stepped a man.

The man was old beyond years and yet looked as young and fresh as a spring flower. His face had no wrinkles and yet was chiseled like a mountain. His face had deep crevasses that contained mysteries and secrets. His hair was white like wool and had the same appearance as the burning white fire in the Seraph. The man's eyes sparkled like colored gemstones and diamonds in a river. They looked like they contained all the stars, suns and galaxies put together, but multiplied by a billion times a trillion. In his right hand he held the globe of the earth beneath a fluffy leather cover. Zoe studied the leather skin. It was the pelt of a lamb! The white wool covered and protected the precious globe beneath. The man held the globe of the earth with great tenderness and affection. In his left hand he held a star. It shone with the radiance and brilliance of a thousand suns. It was beautiful.

Smiling, Father God held out his left hand that held the beautiful star. "This is my most precious treasure," he said. "I give you my Morning Star."

Zoe's knees began to wobble again. Of all the treasures that the Father had, he was giving her his most prized one. She had never imagined that Father God would be like this; so generous, wise and so kind.

Zoe reached out her hand, trembling, to accept the precious gift. She could feel heat radiating from it. It was alive! She hesitated, not sure of what to do. She looked up at Father God and he smiled at her reassuringly. She reached out and took the Morning Star.

An explosion of light pierced Zoe and she was momentarily blinded. When she could see again the star had grown and filled her entire vision. The beautiful star radiated light in every direction. It filled the entire universe with its light and life. She could still feel Father standing next to her, but her gaze was now on the Morning Star.

"I am the Beginning and the End, the Light and Truth of the world," the rich deep voice resonated out from within the depths of the Star.

That voice, she had heard it before! Yes! The glorious light softened slightly. She was able to see into the light. It was Jesus! The light radiating out from him saturated Zoe until she too began to glow. As Zoe gazed upon Jesus' face she was changed to be more like him. She was like a caterpillar being transformed into a beautiful butterfly.

Zoe could see unending kindness in Jesus' eyes. But she also saw deep concern and sadness. Zoe wondered how Jesus, so majestic and glorious, could also look so sad. He picked her up in his arms, kissed her forehead and carried her through what seemed like a corridor. The corridor was like an art gallery. It was lined with hundreds and thousands of portraits on the walls. Some were paintings of a single person, others of families, and there were even groups of people, who for some reason had been painted together. They were all incredibly lifelike. Jesus walked part way down the long corridor. He stopped and carefully put Zoe down in front of one of the groups of paintings. Gray clouds of gloom and despair hung over the people. Some were in pain, and others just looked hopeless and lost. As Zoe looked the paintings changed before her eyes. The transformation was incredible. Hope and joy filled the faces of the people.

"The paintings are of real people on earth," said Jesus. "None of them know me, and they are hopelessly trapped in their situations. I long for them to be set free, to live with me, and my Father forever. The "happy" paintings are how I have really made each person to be, once they know me and overcome. I have brought you to this place for a reason. Find these dear, lost ones, and bring them into my Father's House.

41

I want you to be my hands and feet, eyes and mouth. I want you to rescue them."

Jesus looked very serious. "I have given you many wonderful gifts. You will meet new friends along the way who will help you. Will you go to the place... the place where people end up who don't find me in time?"

Jesus paused, waiting for Zoe's reply. His words carried so much longing and love. Zoe knew that she was being given a very important assignment. However she answered, Jesus would love her just as much as before. Yet she wanted to do her best, to be brave and please him, regardless of any temporary discomfort. "Well... why, YES," she replied. Zoe had learned that when Jesus suggested something it was because it was very important. Even if it appeared scary at first, or difficult, his ways were always best. Jesus could always be trusted one hundred percent. He always meant things for good.

"Thank you, you really are prepared to do all things for me... even if they are brand new things." Jesus knelt down, without shifting his gaze from Zoe. He opened up the palm of his hand and said, "Climb on board."

Zoe stepped into Jesus' open hand. It expanded to fill the whole room and it cradled and surrounded her like a snuggly nest. She felt extremely safe. She looked down and saw her name engraved into the palm of his hand.

"Every time I see my hand I see your name," Jesus said. "I'll never let you out of my sight. I'll be with you until the end of the Age."

The next moment Jesus' hand closed around her. The fingers were strong, and protective. Suddenly she was pressed down into his palm. With incredible force Zoe felt herself being hurled into the air like a rocket. She burst through the earth's atmosphere at supersonic speed. Out into space she flew, past stars and galaxies, travelling faster and faster. An explosion of color, flashing, blinding, amazing lights... Zoe could now make out something like the sphere of the earth again. She had gone in a circle. Now she was passing through a cloud layer— like puffy white candy floss. The circumference of the earth was beautiful, like a precious jewel. But her awe suddenly turned to terror as Zoe plummeted towards it. *I wonder how I am going to brake and land,* she thought. *I don't have a parachute!* A tiny dot became a looming city within moments. Zoe hurtled towards the city at breakneck speed. She could now see rooftops, freeways, and suburbs. She braced herself for the impact. *"Emergency drill: place your hands behind your neck, lean forward, head between your knees...should the oxygen mask appear before you..."* flashed through her mind. Like a meteor Zoe fell from the sky.

Chapter 7

THE PARTY

"What are you doing on the floor all hunched up?" a voice yelled.

Zoe unrolled from her crash position and slowly got up. It took a few moments to get her bearings. Music blared. Pulsating lights flashed through the darkness illuminating the room. It was full of partying people, dancing and drinking. She was back on earth. This was no party in heaven. Heaven parties were wild but always full of joy and God's holiness. This one did not feel like that! It was horrific.

No one seemed to mind or even notice that she had "dropped in" from nowhere: except for the boy standing next to her. They were all preoccupied with pleasures the party offered. Someone thrust a drink of some kind into her hand and said, "Wanna dance?" She politely declined, stepping backwards to escape the advances of the young man. "I need to go to the bathroom," she replied, which was an honest answer, and the first thing that came to mind. Zoe was desperate to escape.

Zoe loved people and adventures. But parties with lots of alcohol and blaring music were not her thing. She could feel the sadness of Holy Spirit inside of her. He was yearning and reaching out for all these lost ones. This was a poor substitute. He was offering them the real deal that would have brought them freedom and life.

The music changed tempo. Zoe managed to maneuver her way out of the living room and into the corridor. She had to step over the sprawled bodies on the floor and squeeze past the draped ones on the sofa. The scene in the hall was no improvement. The kids looked like they had come from all walks of life. There were Middle Eastern kids, Hispanic ones, Afro-Americans, and Europeans; you name it, they were here. It was like a giant melting pot of humanity converging in one place. They were dressed in the latest styles from street to the slickest night club fashions. They had come for one reason only—to have fun!

The corridor didn't provide any hint of having a front or back door, or any way out. Instead it just seemed to offer more rooms full of kids partying. Part of Zoe wondered, *what is wrong with this? What's wrong with letting go and enjoying yourself?* In desperation she managed to find what looked like a bathroom. *At least I'll be safe here until I think of a way out,* she thought. Zoe closed the bathroom door behind her, and instinctively turned the lock. *Now what do I do?* She thought.

Zoe heard a muffled groan near the toilet, before she could gather her thoughts. A boy of about fifteen years was hunched over the floor, clutching his head. He sensed the presence of Zoe in the room, and turned to look at her. His eyes were glazed and unfocused. The expression on his face was blank. The boy looked at Zoe as though trying to remember something. A needle lay on the floor next to him.

Drugs, thought Zoe. Normally she would have turned and left the room. But something about the way the boy looked and his desperation made her hesitate. He was one of the people that she had seen in the paintings. She was not here by chance!

Chapter 8

THE BOY

C ompassion welled up in Zoe as she continued to watch the boy. She desperately wanted to help him. The boy tried to stand, but was unsuccessful. He lurched forward. Zoe stretched out her hand to grab him, but was unable to support his weight, and they both fell. The boy grabbed his stomach, retched, and then vomited all over her. The stench of the vomit was indescribable.

Revolted, she had no further heroic desires and turned away, wanting to flee the room. A thought flashed through her mind: *I have sent you to bring home my long lost children. Will you be a deliverer?* Zoe began to weep. What could she possible do? This kid was clearly out of it. Maybe she could get someone to help by dialing 911, and get an ambulance or something…?

The atmosphere in the room suddenly changed. Zoe's spiritual eyes were opened. It was like a cover had been rolled away from her eyes. Now she could see what was really going on. Hideous demons surrounded the boy. They tugged chains that were attached to the boy's throat, arms and legs. He cried out with each malicious yank. His body was racked with pain. Terrified, he started screaming.

"I see them, I see them. They're coming to get me. Nooo, you can't have me," he shrieked, as he tried to kick one of the demons away. His foot passed right through the demon, and had no effect on it. The demon squealed with delight at the boy's anguish.

Oh, what can I do? Zoe thought frantically. *He's being tortured.* She had seen the beginning of a few horror movies, where crucifixes or garlic were used, but had quickly turned them off. She needed something more powerful than superstition if she was going to be able to help the boy. *If only Jesus were here,* she thought.

You'll never be alone and I'll never leave or forsake you, flashed through her mind. Zoe held up the palm of her hand and smiled. *Yes!* She thought; *Jesus is here with me now. I'm his hands and legs...* "Jesus, what should I do?"

"Tell the boy about me."

"Jesus can help you," she shouted at the boy. "He can heal anyone. All you have to do is ask him. It's really that easy," she pleaded. "He died on the cross for you. He took all of your mistakes and muck-ups so you can get things sorted. That's what you need to do, to say sorry, and ask him into your life. You can go to heaven, and be with him always. He can also heal you now from these drugs, or whatever is happening to you. Just do it! Say it: sorry!"

The words about Jesus gushed out of Zoe like a river in flood. She hoped that she was getting the words right and saying everything that needed to be said.

The boy's response startled her. He started screaming: "No, no," and then his screams changed to muffled sobbing. "I see them, I see them. They're coming." He was now drenched with sweat. His body went rigid. He then suddenly started shaking with violent convulsions. "Get away from me you filthy demons," he screamed.

Zoe shouted. "You shall not have him!"

The demons retreated a few feet away from Zoe; they could not stand to be near her. Her body began to glow from the fire of the Holy Spirit that had erupted inside of her. God was passionate about this kid. The boy's expression changed. He started to laugh hysterically, and then stopped. He moaned, shook, went rigid, and started laughing again. Zoe took his hand and gripped it tightly.

"Jesus can help you. All you have to do is ask him," she gasped into his ear. The boy muttered something, and then went deathly still. "Thank you God that's over," panted Zoe, still recovering from the ordeal.

But something wasn't right. A large sheet of blackest black appeared above them. It floated down and totally covered them. The stench was revolting. It smelled like rotten eggs or decaying fish. The black sheet covered her throat and she started choking. It descended over her shoulders and down the rest of her body. It was cold as ice. She couldn't move or breathe, and finally passed out, unconscious.

Chapter 9

THE SHOP

Zoe awoke. She was standing on a long gray road. It was twilight, neither day nor night. Gloom and despair hung in the air all around her. *At least I can breathe again*, she thought, clearing her throat to make sure there was no obstruction to make her choke again. She looked around. She was not alone. Multitudes of people walked along the road, some of whom she knew. Everyone went in the same direction, down the sloping road. The road had on and off ramps like a freeway. A lot of people joined the group, but hardly anyone was taking the off ramps. The boy from the party was nowhere to be seen.

I wonder what I should do now, Zoe thought. She remembered a lesson from the eagle; when you are not sure of which direction to go, or what to do, the best choice is to wait until Jesus tells you what to do. Zoe stood and listened, walked a bit, and then waited. It was a very strange place.

The road stretched in both directions further than Zoe could see. At the sides of the road, curved walls rose up to form a tunnel. The light was too dim though to see them clearly. Along one side there appeared to be shops, but the store fronts seemed to suck in the pale gray light rather than having any neon signs. Zoe wondered what was so appealing that was making people go inside. She thought that it was OK to investigate further, and followed the crowd. It was strange. She could feel energy, like invisible hands, pulling and drawing her into a shop. Puzzled, Zoe froze.

"In Jesus' name I break all cords, ropes and chains of evil," Zoe commanded. Instantly, something resembling green rope fell off her waist and ankles, hissed on the ground and disappeared in a puff of green smoke. She was no longer compelled to go into the shop. Now she felt free to go in by her own choice and did so. Zoe instinctively looked up as she walked through the door. There were demons stuck to the ceiling like spiders! They were throwing gray colored sacks over every person who entered the shop. You could still make out the people's features through the transparent sacks. The demons saw Zoe and scuttled aside, trembling with fear at her presence.

Zoe walked cautiously further inside the shop. She sat down in one of the empty chairs that surrounded a table in the center of the room. A young lady turned excitedly to Zoe as she sat down.

"This is so wild. I love crystal ball gazing. I got my tarot card reading done the other day too."

The young lady then turned her attention back to a shrouded figure, hunched over the table. The lights dimmed, and a drum roll was piped through hidden speakers, somewhere in the room. "Mystic Mary will now reveal your future," chanted a voice through the same concealed speakers. With a grand gesture, a hooded figure seated at the end of the table dramatically whipped away her head covering. A gasp went up from the audience.

"My, she's so pretty," said a young lady seated near Zoe, who just looked at her stunned. Obviously, she wasn't seeing the same person as the young lady who had just made the comment. The hunched up figure of "Mystic Mary" looked hideous! She had long curled black fingernails, and a matching hooked nose. Worst of all, a nest of snakes writhed around in her hair. Just looking at this woman made Zoe feel quite sick.

"Let the show begin," chanted the prerecorded announcement.

Zoe had seen enough. She no longer felt the need to remain any more. *But all these people in the room are being hoodwinked, and can't see the evil before them*, she thought. Godly revulsion rose up inside her at the deception.

It was then that Zoe noticed a little girl, about half her age, directly opposite her. She did not have one of the gray sacks over her head. Unlike the other people in the room, the little girl was focused and alert. She stood out from the others. Light glowed all around her. Suddenly the light intensified. She slowly raised her hands and began to sing. The song was beautiful and full of power. Crackling flames of fire could be heard above the song. Fire then burst out above her head. This fire, this light, and the holiness and purity of the girl, was the same thing she had felt when she was in the Lord's presence. The little girl was a Christian too!

Zoe began to hum in time to the song. She tapped her feet on the floor and her fingers drummed the rhythm on her chair. The same song as the one the little girl sang welled up inside of Zoe and she too began to sing. Louder and louder the two girls sang. It was a song of warfare and deliverance. The flames of fire above the little girl's head grew larger. Lightning flashed around the room. Powerful angels suddenly invaded the room with drawn swords. The song increased in tempo. Words of victory over God's enemies poured out of the two girls' mouths. The angels' actions matched what was being sung, activated by the words of victory. Strongholds of darkness came tumbling down. The angels sliced off the gray sackcloth from the people's heads with their swords. The atmosphere changed as each person was set free. Brilliant beams of light pierced the gloom. Before long, the room was ablaze with light and glory. The people were transformed, and the captives set free. Something like scales fell off their eyes, and they looked around smiling, as if they had just awoken from a long deep sleep.

The angels then disappeared, as suddenly as they had arrived. Their job was done. The two girls stopped singing. By this stage Mystic Mary was nearly hysterical.

"What have you done, you wicked children?" she screamed. "Ruined, ruined, it's all ruined."

Mystic Mary continued to rant and rave as she thrust herself away from the table, and ran in circles around the room. She looked like she had lost her marbles and didn't know where to find them! She had totally lost the plot. After several frenzied laps of the room, Mystic Mary continued her headless chicken impersonation, ran out the door, and was never seen again—at least by Zoe.

A beautiful fragrance filled the air. Some of the people sat down and gently wept. Others were hugging each other, and some were laughing for joy. The little girl came over to Zoe and took both of her hands.

"Thanks so much for helping," said the little girl beaming. "My name is Cindy. Before I came here Jesus showed me in a vision how he wanted to set these people free. He said that I couldn't do it by myself. He promised that he'd send someone with his heart to help me. Thank you for coming."

Zoe was amazed at how clever Jesus was. He knew about every situation, and how to fit all the jigsaw puzzle pieces together, just at the right time. She thought that sometimes she could see bits of the puzzle. "I guess that's why we need each other," replied Zoe.

Cindy let go of Zoe's hand and gave her a huge hug. "I've been longing for this day," she replied. "Now the real fun can begin!"

"What do you mean?"

"Now that they are free, they need to be looked after. It's no good freeing someone from a cage only to have them fall into the next trap around the corner. They need to learn to care for themselves, and for each other, and then..." she continued with a sparkle in her eyes, "they can set others free as well."

Cindy truly had an evangelist's heart. She loved going into situations and just seeing Jesus blow the darkness apart, and set the captives free.

Just then there was a knock on the door. "Hi, I'm Mike," a voice said. In stepped a portly youth of about seventeen years old. He was dressed in ripped jeans and a faded black tee-shirt. His smile seemed as wide as his girth. He probably wasn't the hero prince type who would leap in and rescue you from the dragon. He was more the guy you would ask where the best pizzas were.

Mike looked around. "Awesome, you two," he said, as he gave them a high five. He then emptied the contents of his bulging rucksack onto the table. Somehow he had a way of providing everyone's favorite food. Zoe wasted no time in helping herself, as it all looked so delicious. While everyone was eating, Cindy and Mike told stories about how Jesus had been leading them. Cindy shared about "getting sorted out", about the cross, and about how asking Jesus to be saved was the only way to get the ticket to heaven. Mike was wandering around praying for people, and just checking that everyone was OK.

When everyone had finished eating, Cindy asked who wanted the heaven ticket. More people were freed from addictions like drugs and alcohol and even someone from nightmares. Everyone asked for Jesus and the heaven ticket. There was lots of happy shouting and laughter. Someone thought they could hear the angels rejoicing. Mike found a bathtub in one of the back rooms of the shop and every new

Jesus friend was baptized straight away, clothes and all. It was party time!

Zoe was wondering what her part was in all of this, when Mike came up to her. "Wanna join in," he asked, "and help pray?" To Zoe's surprise and delight an amazing thing happened! As soon as she started to pray, prophetic words of life and destiny gushed out of her. She "knew things" about the people, although she had never met them before. God just showed her. She spoke out details of what had happened to them, and how God saw each person. Her words brought comfort and healing. *I'm made for this—isn't God wonderful?* Zoe thought, as the river of God flowed out of her. She even found other kids who had a similar prophetic calling to hers. Each person was so different. No two people were alike. Zoe marveled at how unique each person was, and how precious they were to God. Each person was one piece in God's grand jigsaw puzzle, which made up his beautiful Bride.

After Zoe had finished praying, she knew that it was time to be going. She still had her mission to complete; namely, finding the boy who had overdosed in the bathroom. Cindy likewise said that she had some "other stuff to do." Mike though, seemed very happy to stay with his new friends. He was in his element! *They definitely won't go hungry,* thought Zoe with a smile.

Zoe set out down the road again. She knew that she was getting closer to finding the boy. She was certain too, that it wasn't just about finding him, but that Jesus was trying to show her something really important at the same time.

Chapter 10

THE ANGELS AND
THE RED DOOR

The road down the tunnel got narrower and steeper. More and more people entered it. Some entered from the on ramps, and others came out from the buildings. Hardly anyone took the exits. *It's strange,* thought Zoe, *the exit ramps have a radiance and glow to them that make them look inviting and refreshing.* Signposts lined the street: "Find the Creator of all life," "Discover the truth about eternal life," "Live free from guilt and sin," and "Fullness of joy." Yet the people did not notice the messages on the signs. They were fixated on reaching the end of the road. *How could they be so blind?* thought Zoe.

Zoe shuddered. She had reached what she thought must be the end of the tunnel. Cold shivers ran up and down her spine. The place felt very evil. Yet Holy Spirit urged her to keep going. The answer to finding the boy lay out there beyond the end of the tunnel.

Wide steps were chiseled into the rock where the road stopped. Weeds and thorns grew out between the cracks.

The rock itself was worn smooth from millions of people who had taken the path over the centuries. All around her, the people pushed and shoved, as though they couldn't get down the steps fast enough. With each step that Zoe took downwards, the temperature dropped. Foul odors and gases leached through the cracks in the tunnel wall. Desperation lined the faces of the people. Yet Zoe could partly see them with God's heart of compassion. Each person had so much promise of greatness and beauty. She caught a glimpse of the calling of God on each person. She could also feel their pain and struggles, and sensed the tugging and warring in their hearts, as the tunnel drew them down like a magnet.

A light flashed to Zoe's right. She felt heat and turned. Four angels in burning, radiant light stood before her. They shone like the sun in the midday sky. Their golden armor gleamed with the radiance and brightness of ones who had been in the presence of the Lord. Amazingly, hardly anyone seemed to notice them. A few people turned to look at them, paused, and then just kept going down the steps. Fewer still changed direction and approached the angels. Zoe made straight for them. They were even more mighty and glorious up close. They had no wings and were awesome. *They're about four stories high*, thought Zoe. Determination lined the faces of the angels. They stood shoulder to shoulder, swords drawn, and ready for battle. *At any moment they will leap into action,* she thought. But the angels continued to stand their watch, guarding and waiting.

Between the legs of each towering angel was a door that was hinged to the rock wall. The four doors were simply made of panels of wood, and each door was a different color. The red one was the most popular with the few people that were passing through. This door looked ancient, with its faded and peeling paint. All the doors were only about chest height. Each person had to crouch down very low and then crawl through. Zoe thought: *This red door must be the most important as so many are choosing it.* So she followed the others. She got down on her hands and knees, peered through the doorway, and crawled through.

Chapter 11

THE ARMORY

S and crunched beneath Zoe's hands and knees as she made her way through the red door. "Ouch!" Zoe exclaimed, as she quickly got to her feet to avoid the sand that had suddenly got extremely hot. She looked around and found herself in a vast desert of rock and sand. The sun blazed overhead. Angels greeted others as they came through the doorway. This time the angels were human sized ones, and led the people to chariots and camels. A squadron of angels came over to Zoe. They had the same resolute expression and sense of urgency as the giant angels on the other side of the door. Expectantly, they bowed to her and said; "Welcome mighty heroine."

Zoe was puzzled why the angels were bowing to her, and simply nodded. She wasn't sure if she should bow back or not, or maybe curtsey. She had seen someone curtsey once at a ballet she went to with her mom. The angels seemed to be waiting for Zoe to speak. Not really knowing what she should say, she looked around uncomfortably.

"Greetings and welcome, mighty warrior," said one of the angels from the company.

"Hello," Zoe replied, and then continued; "Why are you here?"

"We're waiting for you to tell us what you need, and why you are here. We were sent to serve you, and help you carry out the Father's will. Didn't Holy Spirit lead you here, and tell you what you need to do, for the next part of your quest?"

"Well no," she stammered. "I, well...sort of, well...just followed the others, as this door looked the most important and popular."

The angel studied Zoe intently. He turned to the others who spoke with him in hushed tones. Turning back to her he replied, "We have been assigned to serve all of the Lord's children, as he sends them along this path. As you're here now, it's our responsibility to help you. We will serve you with all our might and ability, so that you can continue what the Lord has given you to do."

Zoe relaxed. She realized that she had been holding her breath, and scrunching up her shoulders as though she was about to be told off. She knew then that she had missed the best choice, by choosing to take the red door. She had compromised by wanting to fit in with the others, instead of simply asking Jesus which door to take. Zoe hoped that her mistake would not cost the boy she was desperately trying to find. Would Jesus forgive her?

"Can I simply go back through the red door, and ask Jesus which is the right way to go?" Zoe asked.

"It's not that simple," replied one of the angels. "Once here, you can't go back the same way. You must now find the best route to take you back to the other doors."

"What is this place, and what is the best way out?" Zoe asked disappointedly. She hoped she was asking the right questions now, as she had made so many mistakes.

"You are inside the armory." The angel who answered was smiling at her, and looked very wise. Zoe noticed that, although all the angels looked very similar, they were all slightly different. They wore markings and insignia, and colorful garments over their golden armor. The armor was brightly polished and gleamed in the desert sun. Zoe wondered how they could walk so effortlessly, as their armor must have been very heavy. Each angel had a long silver sword that glowed with a bluish light. Colorful feather plumes adorned their helmets. Shields were strapped to their backs. They walked with dignity and purpose. Their whole being was one of reverence and admiration for the One they served—the Lord. Each angel seemed to complement the other, and they worked together as a wonderful team, serving and helping.

"What is the armory?" Zoe asked.

"It's a place created by the Father. People like you can come and be refreshed, and equipped for the next part of their journey. You can also get new battle strategies and weapons," replied the angel.

"How do I know what I need?"

"That depends on the assignment you have been given," said another angel closest to Zoe. "Only the Lord can decide what is best for you in each situation. He is the Lord of Hosts and can see from the beginning to the end. He knows all the possibilities that can happen in between."

One of the other angels continued: "That's why the Lord loves using children. They're part of his secret, mighty army. He uses the things that appear weak and foolish to confuse the wise. When children realize how God really sees them, well... he will demonstrate his power and love through them. Strongholds of darkness will be destroyed and multitudes will come to know him. He will pour out healings and miracles through them. It's not the age of the children that's important, but their childlike hearts of love and their trust in him. Mountains will be moved! The children know they need him. He will set them free to minister alongside the grownups."

The angels surrounded Zoe and raised their shields over her head, protecting her from the sun's heat as they walked through the desert. It reminded her of being in a tall forest. Just being in their presence made her feel refreshed and full of faith. Zoe could see other groups of angels also moving in the same direction. Each of the groups carried a tall banner that fluttered in the gentle breeze. The banner that her angels carried was red with the crest of a lion in gold.

They hadn't walked far when they came to a steep ravine. A well-worn path with steps cut into the rock lead downwards. Zoe was glad the angels were with her. The path was very steep and winding. Just looking down made her feel a bit nervous, as she didn't really like heights. At the bottom of the ravine was a narrow stream. Slowly the company made their way down. Zoe kicked off her shoes and stuck her feet into the refreshing water. The angels stood next to her and patiently watched. They did not appear to suffer from the desert heat. Zoe jumped in, splashing about, enjoying the cooling water. *What was that?* Something gleamed on the bottom of the stream. She reached down and pulled out a gold ring.

"I wonder how that got here and who it belongs to," Zoe asked, holding up the ring to the angels.

One of the angels reminded her that the armory was a place of equipping, and that each person was provided with what they needed. Zoe had expected that any new gifts would come from a treasure chest or a big vault, not out of a stream! But then God was not predictable, and did things his own way.

"The ring is for you," continued the angel. "It's to remind you of the Lord and how he made you. You have been fashioned and changed, like this ring, through the heat of trials and pressures you have been through. You are like this beautiful ring in his sight. He looks at you with pleasure and delight. No matter what you face, the Lord's covenant and promises are with you forever. This is a wedding ring — a sign that he has married you! This happened the moment you said "yes" to being his; the day you asked for forgiveness, and chose to follow him. You are his beloved Bride. He will cherish and protect you always."

"What's a covenant?"

"The covenant is what Jesus did for you on your behalf when he died on the cross, rose from the grave, and went to heaven. It's God's permanent agreement between him and you, which lasts forever. When you accepted Jesus as your Lord and Savior, he was bound by the promises that he made. This ring will be a reminder of his love, and that you belong to him."

Zoe ran her fingers over the ring. She could feel the fine engravings. She held it up to get a better look. Hebrew words encircled it. The angel said that her name and one of the names of God were engraved on the ring. There was even the date and time that she had accepted Jesus as her Bridegroom; when she gave her life to him, and asked for her sins to be forgiven.

Joyfully, Zoe slipped the ring onto her finger. The angels helped her out of the water, and waited while she put her shoes and socks back on. They turned towards the mountain. One of the angels pointed to a nearby rock overhang. "You must go inside the mountain," he said.

Chapter 12

THE EMERALD JUNGLE

C ompared to the sunlit stream, the rock overhang cast a shadow that was like night. Zoe raised her hands expecting to feel the stony side of the mountain, but she could see nothing except the blackness. Zoe inched forward into the side of the mountain, hands in front of her in case she banged into something. Hesitantly, she walked a couple of steps. She could now see a faint light, a few feet in front of her. She turned around. The angels hadn't followed! She was about to turn back to get them, when a voice said, "We're not permitted to come any further on this part of your journey. But the Lord of Hosts, the Lord your Beloved, is with you."

Hesitating, Zoe turned around and stepped cautiously towards the light. The light got brighter as she got closer and it was tinged with an emerald green color. A few steps later and she was out from beneath the mountain; standing in a jungle glade. She was surrounded by ancient trees, and lush vegetation—palms and ferns carpeted the jungle floor. The trees were gnarled, stately giants, which soared up into the sky, their branches almost touching the clouds! They must have been hundreds of years old. Luxurious vines covered in honey colored, perfumed flowers were suspended high overhead like an amazing Broadway set. Shafts of sunlight punctuated the emerald green canopy, and Zoe could see dragonflies and hummingbirds darting to and fro.

Zoe was wondering what she should do next, when she heard the soft crunch of feet making their way towards her, through the jungle undergrowth. She sighed with a sigh of relief, as a new company of angels stepped into sight, in front of her.

"Welcome favored one" they said," we've been expecting you."

This company too was clad in the same heavenly armor as the other angels whom she had been with. Yet the clothing of these angels was different from the others. Perhaps it was the combinations of colors, or perhaps the patterns. Whatever the difference, these angels too were very pleased to see her.

"We must hurry," said one of the angels. "Come with us."

They quickly led Zoe through the jungle for several minutes, although she could not make out any path or markings on the jungle floor. The air got steamier. A fine mist formed droplets on the leaves that splotted onto Zoe's face.

I wonder if there are any snakes here, thought Zoe, making sure she kept close to the angels. The source of the fine mist was a large waterfall. It fell a couple of hundred feet into the river below. The river was broad and gentle, despite the power of the cascading waterfall. Water lilies grew just beyond the splash range. Above the roar of the waterfall Zoe could hear something. She looked up and saw a blur of colors: reds, oranges, greens and yellows. The giant canvas of light and color constantly moved, swaying back and forth like a giant swarm of bees. Then it came to rest on one side of the river bank. Thousands of multicolored parrots had landed to drink from the sweet, clear water. They didn't mind Zoe or the angels being there. Refreshed, they rose into the air like a beautiful Persian carpet, and flew off into the jungle. Zoe smiled. She knew the parrots she had set free from the golden cage were now part of this wild flock.

The angels had also enjoyed watching the wild parrots. But as soon as the parrots left, they hurriedly continued their journey. The river was swifter beyond the clearing and the waterfall. It was lined with even bigger and more ancient trees than before, stronger than oaks and more majestic than cedars. Their canopies were immense. They were laden with fruits and flowers all at the same time. *Very unusual*, thought Zoe, who enjoyed helping her dad in the garden. She knew that the flowers usually came first, and then the fruit. Not everything all at once! *This is a most unusual place*, she thought.

The angels took Zoe to one of the enormous trees. Some kind of ladder or staircase wound its way up the gigantic tree. Angels were climbing up and down carrying things wrapped in linen and golden cloth. They smiled in recognition at Zoe and the angels with her, but passed by quickly as they delivered their important cargoes.

One of the angels in the company with Zoe said, "The Lord wants to show you something...a very special gift."

Zoe nodded, as if every day she was invited to climb staircases up giant trees. She started her climb. She hadn't gone far when she looked down.

"Don't look back," said one of the angels gravely, "or you may lose your balance and fall off. Keep looking straight ahead, and upwards."

Quickly, Zoe turned around and looked up. The tree was immense. Its leaves, boughs and branches appeared to stretch in all directions. Through time the bark had worn smooth. Zoe smiled. The patterns on the bark and even the leaves had actually grown into shapes that formed words. This tree was a living word tree. The Bible verses rolled off easily over her tongue. Different parts of the tree contained words and stories around themes. She was now passing through the garden and orchard section: "You will be like a well-watered garden, like a tree planted by streams of water which yields its fruit in season and whatever you do, you will prosper."

After a short while, she entered the "Fear not" section: "Have I not commanded you? Be strong and courageous. Do not be terrified; do not be discouraged, for the Lord your God will be with you wherever you go," [2] and "Before I formed you in the womb I knew you, before you were born I set you apart; I appointed you as a prophet to the nations." [3] *Cool,* thought Zoe, *God was right when he said his word was sharper than a two edged sword. He is so full of life. Even creation expresses his word!*

Zoe burst out through the jungle canopy. Still the tree went higher. She could see other trees puncturing the canopy and majestically rising into the air. *Was this what it was like to be a bird soaring, looking down on the world below?* The air at this height was incredibly refreshing. She felt like an eagle, and could see for miles around in all directions.

Chapter 13

SEATED IN
HEAVENLY PLACES

At last they reached the top, just as Zoe felt she had been climbing forever. The staircase suddenly ended. Before her was a large wooden platform, like something from a Treasure Island movie. Everything was made of wood or leaves, lashed together with vines. It was a beautiful place. There were wooden tables, and chairs, and soft cushions made from leaves. There were even rugs that appeared to be made from leaves, stitched and woven together. Everything looked so comfortable. She could imagine spending a lot of time here, just enjoying the view below. It was like the most exotic boutique hotel. But what was even more amazing was the person seated before her. He sat on a large wooden chair...or was it a throne, inlaid with polished shell.

The warmth of Jesus' smile, and the radiance of his eyes, was enough to make her heart melt, or light a thousand bonfires, all at once!

"Oh Jesus," shouted Zoe, as she ran towards him, and threw her arms around his neck.

He did not seem to mind Zoe acting like a long lost puppy finding her master again. Instead, he turned and hugged her back and playfully rolled around on the floor with her, as she continued to snuggle up to him.

Finally Zoe stopped. She looked up into his eyes. They were like deep pools of water and twinkling starlight. "I've missed you so much," she said. "Why did you wait so long before letting me find you?"

"I've always been with you, little one," replied Jesus affectionately, as though she were his favorite friend. "It's just that you haven't been able to see me with your natural eyes until now."

He then led her back to the wooden chair he had been sitting on. There was a smaller one next to his, carved out of the same wood. Zoe's name was engraved on it.

"This is how I see you, seated next to me in heavenly places. Before I show you something else, would you like something to eat? You must be very hungry and thirsty after your long climb."

"Why yes, thank you." Although it was with the help of the angels that she had been able to reach the top, she was very hungry and thirsty indeed. Zoe wondered what Jesus would offer her. She had read in the Bible that John the Baptist ate locusts and honey, and that angels gave the children of Israel manna to eat when they walked through the desert.

Jesus reached out to a nearby branch and pulled it down to Zoe's height. "What is your favorite ice-cream?" he asked.

"Goody-goody gumdrops," she replied expectantly.

Jesus plucked the nearest fruit from the tree. It was pink in color, and he carefully peeled open the skin, before handing it to Zoe. Inside was the most exquisite looking ice-cream. An angel came and gave her a spoon and a waffle. She tucked into it hungrily. The ice-cream was so delicious, cool without making your teeth sore, and full of her favorite flavors. It was gone in the twinkling of an eye. Zoe wondered about asking for more, but already felt quite full, and so decided not to.

Jesus didn't seem to want any himself. He took Zoe by the hand and carefully unwrapped another fruit, filled with several different flavors.

I think I would like to come back here when I'm hungry again, she thought.

The time that followed was full of laughter and stories. Jesus wanted to know how she had found the adventure up until now, what she had learned, and what had been difficult. He kept reassuring her, and saying how proud he was of her. He didn't really seem to mind that she had taken the red door, instead of the green one. He said that although it had delayed part of her journey, it would all be alright in the end. Just like a game of chess, she had made a wrong move, but he would move the other pieces around so that she would win the prize. Zoe liked prizes!

The time spent with Jesus was like the best vacation you could imagine. His presence washed over her like a gently flowing river, reviving and refreshing her. He made her feel so loved and special. She felt like his favorite friend. She knew that no mountain was too high to climb, or valley too deep to cross. With Jesus nothing was impossible.

The sun was beginning to set. Zoe could see the morning star rise above the horizon. Jesus placed a blanket around her shoulders, and led her to the edge of his tree-house.

"The light shines brightest in the darkest places," he said. "I am the light of the world sent out by our Father to drive out the darkness. I have overcome the darkness." Jesus pointed with his right hand to the earth below as he spoke.

Zoe could make out what looked like pillars of fire and light rising up through the jungle canopy like search light beacons. Other areas were so dark that she shuddered.

"The beacons of light are places where people, communities, and cities have asked me to be Lord of their lives. The areas of darkness are the places where people don't want me, or have never heard about me," explained Jesus sadly. "Every time someone hands their life over to me the fabric of time and space is also transformed. My light and presence comes inside that person and shines out through them."

"What about the people who don't want you?" enquired Zoe tentatively.

Jesus paused, and then looked at her. His sadness almost made her cry. It was the sadness of someone who longs for something beyond what words can describe.

"The ones who reject me will spend all eternity separated from me and from my Father's love. I don't want to lose any of them, but I always honor their choices."

"If they become separated from you, can't they choose you once they realize?" asked Zoe, not being able to imagine how anyone could or would want to reject him.

"There are boundaries and conditions set in place by my Father. Once a person leaves the earth and dies, it is too late to ask me to be saved, and be Lord of their life. I give every person many opportunities to accept me while they are living. If they don't do this while alive...well...after that there is only eternal separation."

Jesus put his hand on Zoe's shoulder.

"I want you to do something very special for me. I have made and chosen you, along with many other children, to do wonderful things in my name. I want you to help save the children who are perishing. But rather than just tell you something, I want to show you firsthand so that you will always remember."

Zoe looked into Jesus' eyes. His look of longing for those that didn't yet know him was almost unbearable. This was his pain that he carried, until every last breathing person on the face of the planet knew him and made their choice, and could be presented to his Father as his precious Bride.

Everything in Zoe wanted to run away, yet how could she? If she truly loved Jesus she would do anything for him. After pleasing the Father, this was the most important thing for him in the entire universe.

"Yes," she replied feebly, almost choking on the words.

Jesus bent down. He plucked a flower about the size of the palm of her hand. It was the same kind that she had seen growing in the doll's house conservatory—a red passion-flower. It was darker and redder than the one she had seen earlier. He placed the flower over her heart. Immediately a flame of fire shot out of it and penetrated deep into the core of her body. She could feel the imprint of the flower, fire and passion burning deep into her spirit. Without talking, Jesus took her hand, and led her over to the edge of the platform. Something like a circular hole in the floor had been cut out. Zoe looked into the hole, but could only see darkness. Gently Jesus pushed her towards the hole. She could have resisted, but didn't. He wanted her to step in! She knew it was time to go.

Jesus reached down, kissed Zoe on the forehead and squeezed her hand reassuringly. The last she saw of him was the wide smile of delight on his face. "Thank you my beloved," he said. Zoe let go of his hand, and stepped into the blackness.

Chapter 14

THE LIGHT SHINES IN THE DARKNESS

Zoe was engulfed by darkness. A wave of cold air smacked into her face like a sheet of ice. Her arms and legs splayed in all directions as she desperately tried to find the ground. But there was none. She tumbled down into the abyss.

Why didn't I ask for a parachute? she thought. *That was silly.*

She fell like a stone. There was a faint blur as she passed by what might have been lights, as she tumbled downwards. Zoe's head ached.

Surely I should have reached the ground by now...I've been falling so long. Still, she kept falling.

Perhaps I've dropped into a large crevasse inside a mountain, or will wake up at any moment from a bad dream. Oh, I do hate these falling dreams! I hope I don't end up falling out of my bed and end up on the floor.

Suddenly, she stopped falling. One minute she was plummeting full throttle—the next she was standing upright on her feet. The nausea left her, but she could still see nothing.

Deepest night surrounded her. Not a star or the moon could be seen. Zoe stretched out her hand as she stepped forward. She tried to find the edge of the room, or a tree; in case she was still in the jungle. She took several steps and still found no solid object. She paused. The hair on the back of her neck stood up. Someone else was there. She was being watched like prey being stalked by a hunter.

"Jesus where are you?" she shouted.

"Don't ever mention that n-aaa-me," a voice hissed somewhere over to her left. Zoe's body began to feel numb, as she felt the evil presence draw nearer.

"This one's mine," another voice crackled. "Leave her to me."

Zoe spun around. There was nowhere to go, nowhere to hide. The temperature dropped, and her teeth started chattering with the cold.

"Jesus I need you. You said you'd never leave or forsake me," she prayed. But there was no miraculous rescue, no angelic intervention. Yet, Zoe felt peace rise up inside of her like a river surging up in flood. Peace saturated her whole being. It was as if icicles had been broken off her heart, and she could move again.

"Use what I have given you," she heard Holy Spirit in her mind, prompting her.

Zoe's thoughts went to the ring that she had been given. She remembered how precious Jesus said she was to him, and that his light had overcome the darkness.

"The Lord is my light and salvation -- whom shall I fear," she boldly proclaimed. [4]

Instantly rays of pulsating light shot out from the ring in all directions.

"Jesus is the Morning Star," she continued to proclaim.

The light from the ring blazed like the sun. There was a scuttling sound. Hideous creatures that looked transparent, like jello, panicked and tried to find cover from the piercing light. But there was no place to hide from its brilliance. They were standing on a vast plain that stretched as far as the eye could see. It was shiny like ice and featureless. The jello creatures had something resembling arms and legs which were long and exaggerated. Their faces were hideous, and looked tormented as if they were locked in their own nightmare, too. The creatures dragged themselves away from the light as fast as their gangly legs allowed them to. Zoe looked up and saw a vast vaulted ceiling covered in stalactites. They hung like knives ready to fall. The light from the ring continued to burn brightly. *What now Lord, where do I go?*

"Onwards and forwards," she heard Holy Spirit say in her mind.

Zoe gazed around the featureless icy plain. It looked like it stretched forever in every direction. The light of the ring continued to burn with a fierceness that drove the darkness away. But Zoe knew it was only temporary. As she moved, the light of the Lord's presence moved, and shone out through her. This place was darkness itself, and when she left she knew the darkness would return.

Zoe remembered her sword, which the Lord had commanded her to eat. She said, "Your word is a lamp to my feet and a light to my path." [5] Instantly, words appeared in the air where she had spoken. Then, the words floated to the ground. When they touched the cold ice-like earth, a golden path formed in front of her. It was not a large path. It was only about one to two feet wide, and seven feet long, but perfect for her needs. Zoe stepped on to it full of faith, and expectancy. A miracle happened! With every step that she took; the path grew just one step longer, right before her eyes. She looked back. The path had disappeared, as though it knew its purpose had been completed. Zoe boldly stepped forward. Sure enough, the golden path kept appearing in front of her.

This can only be God, she thought, as she followed the path through the wasteland.

Chapter 15

INTO THE
JAWS OF DEATH

*T*his place can't be heaven, thought Zoe, as she continued to walk. *It's more grotesque than anything I've imag-ined on earth, even worse than the scariest horror movie* (and she didn't like horror movies at all!).

Zoe had no idea how long she walked. She faithfully kept going as long as the path in front of her kept appearing. She could sense the Lord's presence all around her, although she couldn't see him. She knew that she was not alone. Fortunately, the jello demons hadn't returned. Zoe shud-dered just remembering them, and decided not to even try and figure out what they were.

At last there appeared to be an end to the vast plain before her, or at least something different than the flat sea of ice. A jagged outcrop of what Zoe could only describe as an ice-cliff rose up from the ground. It appeared as tall as a six story building, but it was difficult to get a sense of scale in this place. The light from the ring illuminated the rock outcrop. It was jet black. Where the light fell on the rock, it seemed to be absorbed right into the rock-like substance.

Zoe would have gladly passed by the rock face, but the pathway led directly to it. The nearer she approached, the more she could feel fear and a great sadness coming from it.

Zoe didn't know exactly what to do so she opened her mouth instinctively and spoke again. Words formed like fire in front of her; "You will possess the gates of your enemies." She looked up again at the rock face. She could now see it was shaped like a skull and formed a giant gateway. The skull seemed to feed on any life that there was, drawing it into itself. The mouth of the skull hissed as noxious black vapors floated out. The eye sockets glowed with a menacing red light.

I wonder who my enemy is, she thought. Then, she remembered her quest to rescue the boy. Whatever or whoever was holding him captive, must be the enemy. The pathway led right up to the skull's mouth. *Great*, she thought, *I've got to climb inside that thing.*

Suddenly, there was a movement either side of the mouth. Two enormous dog-like creatures about the size of elephants lurched towards her. Instinctively Zoe raised her arm to shield herself. With a "crash" one of the creature's legs smashed into the side of her body. She was thrown to the ground. Miraculously, she was not hurt. The creatures snarled at the sight of her, as if they were frightened.

Strange, Zoe thought, *why're they so frightened? They're at least four times the size of me and could squash me flat.* She had no doubt that was exactly what they wanted to do. *I need a word*, she desperately thought. *Any word, no, the right word.* "Oh Lord, help; which one?" she stammered as she desperately wished she had remembered more of her Bible. "Please God, I'll read the Bible every day when I get back home. I promise."

"Fear not, for I have redeemed you; I have summoned you by name; you are mine. When you pass through the waters, I will be with you; and when you pass through the rivers, they will not sweep over you. When you walk through the fire, you will not be burned; the flames will not set you ablaze. For I am the Lord, your God, the Holy One of Israel, your Savior." [6]

That's a brilliant one, Zoe thought with relief, remembering that she had read it somewhere in Isaiah. But she knew she needed to act quickly so that her actions lined up with the Word. Zoe advanced again. Quickly, before she forgot the Bible verses, she spoke them out. What happened next was totally unexpected. Something started sloshing around in her tummy and making a gurgling sound. The sloshing rose inside of her. She thought she was going to be sick. And then she was!

Zoe vomited out buckets of water. As the water hit the floor, it multiplied and expanded. It formed a huge wave just in front of her — a wall of towering water. The wave paused momentarily as if contemplating its enemy, and then with an almighty "crash" it fell upon the astonished creatures. The sound of the breaking wave reverberated throughout the plain.

The water drained into the ground and disappeared as though it had never been there. The creatures were nowhere to be seen. Perhaps they had been swept away by the wave? But whatever had happened to them; Jesus had saved her, yet again. Still a bit shaken, she walked towards the skull doorway.

Chapter 16

BEYOND
THE SKULL DOOR

The gateway was even more grotesque close up. It seemed to suck all of life into its mouth and then try to extinguish it. It was covered in some sort of slimy substance, which was black like oil that moved and slithered. Zoe peered down more closely and nearly leapt back with disgust. Covering the skull was a crawling mass of thousands of centipede-like insects. She pulled back her hand very fast, so as not to get bitten. If it wasn't for the golden pathway, she would have had to stand on them to get through the entrance. The insects scuttled out of the way to avoid the light. Zoe stepped through the entrance. She could hear her heart beating faster and a trickle of sweat rolled down her face. She held her breath... was it actually getting warmer? Very warm, indeed. A faint red glow got brighter as Zoe walked through the tunnel-like entrance. The light of her ring revealed that the tunnel was very wide, but just how wide she couldn't tell. The walls had large gouges and scratch marks raked along them. Zoe shuddered at the thought of how they had got there. The red glow increased in intensity the further along she walked. The tunnel also grew wider. Zoe neared the tunnel exit. She walked past what once must have been trees. All that remained of them now were wizened, twisted stumps. The wood had become petrified and looked like hard gray stone.

Surrounding the source of the light at the end of the tunnel were massive, two story double doors. They were intricately carved as though a king or queen were going to make a grand entrance. Yet, when Zoe looked at them with the eyes of her heart they were not really beautiful or grand at all, but rather evil and forbidding. She knew that her quest and the destiny of the boy lay beyond those doors. The golden path stopped just short of the doors. They were tightly shut.

There was no door handle or knob to be seen. What was the key to unlocking them?

Her heart pounded. Zoe reached up without thinking and placed her hand over her heart, wondering how she would open the doors. A pleasant warm sensation filled the palm of her hand.

Puzzled, she drew her hand away from her chest. Cupped in her hand was a passionflower. It was the same one she had seen in the doll's house, in the conservatory. She held it up in front of her and turned it around admiringly. It was the exact same shape as the keyhole in the door. Taking the passionflower she pressed it into the keyhole and found that it matched perfectly.

Nothing happened. Disappointed, Zoe stepped back from the door. There was a large grinding sound, like rusted metal that was moving after a very long time of inactivity. The doors slowly swung open.

The force of the wind that struck her nearly knocked her backwards. It was a fierce, hot wind that cut into her face. Zoe braced herself by leaning forwards. Determined, she stepped into the howling wind…

Zoe found herself stepping out into a circular courtyard surrounded by six golden columns. They arched up overhead, meeting at the top, forming a cage. She felt trapped like the parrots she had seen in the golden cage. Instinctively, she reached out and grabbed hold of one of the columns to steady herself, then quickly pulled back her hand. The column was hotter than an oven. Not sure of what to do next, Zoe took another step between the nearest two columns. The wind instantly died down. The air pressure all around her suddenly increased. She felt like she was gripped by a giant vice, and that her life was being squashed out of her body. Surrounding her hundreds of miles high were towering mountains that seemed to be trying to dash her to pieces.

She stumbled backwards into the courtyard of columns again. This was the wrong place to be!

"Jesus, which way should I go?" Zoe shouted into the howling wind. She felt the reassuring presence of Holy Spirit guiding her to go between the fourth and fifth columns. Obediently she threw herself between them.

Chapter 17

ETERNAL FIRE

Tormented screams filled the air. All around her were masses of people writhing and screaming in agony. The whole place was filled with fire and everyone was burning... agonizing fire that burned forever! Flames leapt off the people, and although they were on fire, their flesh kept growing back, and then burning up, so the cycle kept repeating itself. This was Hell: the place of eternal punishment and separation from God. It was more horrible than she had ever imagined. The very things that people had done on earth that were evil were continually tormenting them here. *If people only knew what they really were doing on earth,* thought Zoe. She could not bear to watch as the suffering was so great. She turned away. But there was no escape. Everywhere she looked the place was full of people; jam packed without an inch to spare.

There was no door, no way out. But she was surrounded by the Lord's presence, and the flames could not touch her. Then she remembered his promise: "When you walk through the fire you will not be burned; the flames will not set you ablaze." *So why was she here then? Where was the boy?* Then the awful reality hit her. It was just as the Lord had said in the Bible, that Hell was a real place prepared for those who were disobedient and had rejected him. She would tell as many people as possible and warn them...that is, when she got out!

Zoe looked around. The landscape was littered with bodies everywhere. A stench of something like sulfur filled the air. The ground was shifting and shaking, continuously traumatized by earthquakes. A kind of music was beating, deeper than the groans of the people. But it had no rhythm or melody. It was dreadful. She covered her ears with her hands, but could not drown out the moans of the people or the groaning, rumbling earth.

Then, Zoe remembered her mission. She must find the boy. She could feel the protective presence of Holy Spirit all around her. She knew that what she was experiencing would be too much to bear without him.

A door opened just in front of her. In fell the very boy she was looking for, as if he had been pushed. He looked exactly as he had at the party. All of the color had drained from his face and he was deathly pale. He opened his eyes as if he had just awakened to the nightmare. He screamed.

"Help me, help me. Jesus, Jesus I do believe. I said I do."

Zoe ran to him and flung her arms around him. Desperately, she tried to put out the flames that had started to consume him. It made no difference though. She couldn't extinguish them. Then an amazing thing happened. Something inside Zoe's spirit exploded. She began to glow, hotter than the surrounding fire. She shone with a brilliance brighter than ten thousand suns. Instantly, she knew what had happened. It was Jesus who had given himself to her as the Morning Star. He was inside of her! This was partly what he meant when he said that he would never leave or forsake her. He was expanding and radiating out through her with his glory and power. The radiating glory hit the boy like an atomic bomb explosion. The Lord's presence wrapped around him like a blanket, totally extinguishing the flames.

A beam of light from above cut through the Hell fire like a laser and surrounded them both. They were saturated and gripped by the most incredible light. Instantly they were drawn up out of the pit of Hell, into the glory.

Chapter 18

BENEATH
THE CRYSTAL SEA

S tanding before her, was Jesus. His smile filled the universe. His eyes radiated such love, joy and excitement.

"Well done, my champion," he said.

He then knelt down, took Zoe's hand in his and kissed
her on the head. "My awesome little friend," he said.

"The boy," stammered Zoe, still trying to get her bearings.

"He's safe and being looked after."

Zoe looked around and could see the presence of angels
all around them. Flashes of lightning and fire moved back
and forth amongst the angels as some disappeared to complete some errand, and others arrived. Their presence alone
was intoxicating and made her feel a little giddy. Good thing
Jesus had her by the hand to steady her. Zoe looked down
and noticed that she was walking on water that was crystal
clear yet hard as glass. She could still feel the wetness of
the water beneath her toes. Yet at the same time the water
was actually burning, and fire and smoke arose from it. This
fire was different from the fire she had just experienced in
Hell. The fire was full of the holiness and presence of the

Lord. It was purifying and reviving all at the same time. Zoe was overcome by Jesus' love and refreshed, just by being in his presence.

Together they walked across the crystal sea. How far they walked she did not know—just that it was a journey of pure joy. They did not talk. Zoe soaked in Jesus' presence like a sponge. As they walked, Zoe could see people through the water below on earth. They were going about their everyday life, unaware that they were being watched. The crystal sea was like a giant lens that focused on the vast sea of humanity.

At a specific location Jesus stopped and pointed with his right hand to the earth below, indicating that Zoe should look. She saw a group of people. In the midst of the group was the boy she had helped rescue. There were other teenagers surrounding him. Zoe could hear them speaking.

"It was horrible," gasped the boy. "I was burning up with fire, and I was trapped and couldn't get away."

"It's the drugs," said one of his friends.

"No, no, it wasn't," shrieked the boy, "it was real. I was in Hell."

"Come on Ian," another friend teased. "You've had trips before and this was just another one of them."

"No it wasn't," Ian replied with such a certainty that the others went quiet. "I died and ended up in Hell. I was really DEAD, I know I was there. There was also this girl. She kept going on and on about Jesus... she said I had to ask him for help and for forgiveness. There were also these things— demons, beating me. They had these huge chains around my neck, arms and legs. They were dragging me into some sort of dark pit...it was horrible, all smoking and burning. The girl just kept going on and on about Jesus. I couldn't stand it. I wanted to hit her and make her shut up. But then something about her made me believe she was telling the truth. I could see smoke and fire moving out of the black hole. I was about to be dragged in. I screamed out: "Jesus, forgive me.

94

I believe that you are the Son of God." Suddenly, the next moment I was surrounded by all this fire and I was burning up. I couldn't stop it and I couldn't get away. Then the girl was there too. There was this light that came out from inside her. She burned like a fireball, so bright I could hardly see her anymore. She came up and threw her arms around me. I felt so peaceful, and the painful fire on me stopped. I knew that it wasn't because of the girl. Somehow this Jesus person put the fire out."

Ian paused, as if trying to find the right words.

"I sort of, well, kinda was gripped like with this giant hand. It yanked me out of the darkness and I found myself here."

The other kids looked at Ian, not quite sure what to believe. They were clearly shaken. Ian now looked healthy. His color had returned to his face, his eyes were focused and he breathed normally.

"Come," said Jesus to Zoe, as he placed his hand on her shoulder and led her across the crystal sea.

Chapter 19

DELIGHTED

As they walked, Zoe hardly noticed the people below the water. Her thoughts were on what she had just seen, on Ian, and her part in the rescue. She was amazed. She looked up at Jesus and he smiled at her. She smiled back contently. Zoe knew that when they arrived at their destination there would be plenty of time for questions.

The sea was beautiful. It was so clear and pure. The water was alive with God's presence. His holiness made everything glow with his life. Above the water, the air was as blue as blue could be. The fire continued to burn on the surface of the sea and flickered as they walked through the flames. This fire though, was different from the fire she had seen in the pit. It was fluid like the water, and fluttered like a flag in the breeze. It was full of the Spirit of the Holy One. It was like a dancer celebrating the Creator, as it crackled and burned with joy. In fact, all of heaven was alive, continuously praising and loving him.

They reached the seashore. The beach was golden, like liquid honey. Waves gently lapped onto the sand and reminded Zoe of Jesus' heartbeat. All of the sounds of heaven were perfectly in tune and aligned to their Maker; yet each part of his creation was distinctively different and unique. It was a place of great contradictions and mystery, all held and tied together by this amazing, loving God.

I wonder if this is what it would be like to fully belong to Jesus, wholeheartedly, Zoe thought. *I think it must be. No wonder everything on earth is crying out for his coming, so that it can be restored to the way it was meant to be.*

They walked up the beach to a small wooden shack. It looked like something on a desert island. It was very simple with two windows either side of the door. The wood was worn and aged and if there once was any paint on it, it was long gone. Yet the shack looked very warm and inviting. Jesus indicated that they should step inside, as he pushed open the door to allow her to enter.

The first thing Zoe noticed was the roaring fire. She realized that she had been to this place before! It was the library room—the same one from her first adventure in heaven. It looked exactly as it had done last time: the wall to wall bookshelves, the portraits, paintings and maps and even the oversized cushions and sofas. Last time she was here, her adventure had only just begun. She wondered what Jesus was going to show her this time. He left the room while she looked around. A few moments later he returned. He was carrying a glass of juice and a plate of delicious looking bread. He broke off a piece of the bread and gave it to her. She hadn't realized how ravenous she was. She hungrily washed it down with the large glass of juice. The bread was warm and must have just been baked. The juice tasted like blueberries and wild raspberries, and was totally delicious.

She finished the last of the juice and gasped, nearly dropping the glass. She was covered in flames!

"I'm on fire!"

"It's OK. You've caught the passion that I have for the lost. As long as you seek me with all of your heart you'll burn for the same things I do. My passion for the lost will

burn until the last person on earth has made their choice...
while time still remains."

"What do you mean, while time still remains?"

"This age on earth will end very soon. A new and better
one is about to come. But before it does, my invitation is
open to everyone who wants it. What you experienced in
Hell was a small part of what awaits those who reject me
and my Father's love. For those ones there is only eternal
separation..."

Jesus paused for a moment, looking very sad. He then
looked up at Zoe and smiled.

"I wanted you to see what it was like without me, so that
you could tell others. It's very important that you only go to
those ones I send you to. For every unsaved person I have a
plan for reaching them."

Jesus was watching her to make sure that she understood.
Satisfied that she did, he got up and walked over to one of
the bookcases near the fire. He took out a book, brought it
over to her, opened it up and placed it on her lap.

On the pages were hundreds of names from every country
in the world. There were however some spaces that were
blank. Zoe looked up at Jesus and he nodded.

"Yes, the blank spaces are the dear ones who haven't
yet decided for me. I earnestly watch and wait for them
to make their choice, and have their name written in my
Book of Life."

Jesus pointed to one of the names: "Ian Swanson." *Could
this be the same boy that she had helped rescue?* She looked
up, and Jesus nodded.

"There is room for every person in my Book of Life."
Jesus then took Zoe's hand and placed it on Ian Swanson's
name. She gasped. She could momentarily see into Ian's
life. She knew the plans and destiny that were marked out
for him—the potential that Jesus had placed in his spiritual
DNA. Zoe could see the choices that he would have to make

to grow up to be a mature son of God, to achieve all that he was made to be. She saw the main thing for his life—to worship the Lord, not by doing things but just by being with him. She saw the acts of love and power that were meant to flow though Ian's life as he abandoned himself to God. Zoe was shaken by how the Lord saw Ian.

"The spiritual gifts and calling that I have placed on your life, Zoe, enable you to see how heaven sees things in others. I want you to help others run their race and complete their destinies in me."

Zoe realized that she was seeing Ian through Jesus' eyes as he saw him, not as he was now, but as he was made to be. Ian's mistakes and failures didn't feature in the plan. Jesus only saw the hope, potential and promise. A red shroud or kind of veil that was also transparent covered the boy. Zoe could see through it and read his name in the book.

"Ian is covered by my blood; my covering of grace. All that is confessed and forgiven is covered and remembered no more."

Zoe was tempted to keep her hand on Ian's name. But she knew that the Lord had allowed her a brief look into his life for a fleeting moment to teach her something. She knew that to leave her hand any longer and keep looking would go beyond what she needed to know. She quickly withdrew her hand.

Jesus put his arms around her and gave her a loving hug. "It's right only to look into things I show you. That's why a heart that is pure is so important. Many of the kids drawn to the occult are trying to find out mysteries that I never intended them to know about. Many of these ones are actually called as young prophets. But without the fear of the Lord the very things they are drawn to overtake and control them. My knowledge always has safe limits and boundaries."

Zoe could have remained in this place forever. Jesus' words rolled over her like sweet honey. They refreshed and revived her. She was filled with hope, love and a deep sense of peace and gratitude. But she knew that it was time to go. The adventure for now was almost over.

"You'll come back here many, many times. Sometimes you will come like this. Other times, your spirit will come while you are dreaming on earth and are asleep. I have prepared many wonderful adventures for both of us." Jesus then bent over and tenderly kissed her again on the forehead.

Chapter 20

TO BURN
WITH ETERNAL LOVE

The tender touch of Jesus' lips on her forehead still lingered as she opened her eyes. She looked up, and was surprised to see her brother looming over her. She was dripping wet. Zoe reached out and tried to grab a rock to steady herself from falling over. Sam's splash had made her lose her balance. Her hand brushed her brother as she lurched to the side.

"Ouch," exclaimed Sam, "you burned me."

Zoe looked down at her hands. She couldn't see the fire any more. She closed her eyes and thought about Jesus. All around her she could feel his presence, his longing and his great pleasure for her. Zoe looked up at her brother. A blur of green flashed by out of the corner of her eye. She turned and caught a glimpse of a pair of parrots disappearing into the trees further up the beach. *Freedom*, she thought. Zoe looked back towards her brother, so cool, so sure of himself, and yet not really free at all. She felt her heart begin to burn. She knew exactly what she was supposed to do...!

BIBLE VERSES USED

[1] Isaiah 6:3 NIV
[2] Joshua 1:9 NIV
[3] Jeremiah 1:5 NIV
[4] Psalm 27:1 NIV
[5] Psalm 119:105 NIV
[6] Isaiah 43:1-3 NIV

ABOUT DAN ROBERTSON

Children's stories have always captivated Dan, especially ones where God was involved. As a child he used to dream of being an astronaut, traveling to outer realms of space—little did he know that one day he would meet Jesus and learn that he could experience heaven and see things in the spirit! His life was turned upside down and his view of traditional Christianity exploded when he and his wife experienced new moves of Holy Spirit that were sweeping the globe in the 90s. No longer were dreams, visions, and angelic encounters found only in the Bible, they became alive and real. Refreshed and excited by what God was doing, Dan and his wife became part of an apostolic prophetic team in Europe where they ministered for a number of years.

Dan's wife used to love to hear prophetic bedtime stories the last thing at night before she fell asleep. The better the story the quicker she fell asleep! Sometimes the stories had to be repeated over several nights for Dan's wife to hear the whole thing. The heroine in the stories was always a child who was very brave and very kind, and so Zoe Pencarrow was born.

Dan's heart is to see a passionate generation of children ignited to be radical lovers of Jesus. The seven books in the Zoe Pencarrow series are part of Dan's journey to inspire and awaken the hearts of children and adults to God's amazing love, encouraging them to take hold of their destiny and become all that they are called to be. Dan also works in the marketplace and is involved in issues of social justice.

Lightning Source UK Ltd.
Milton Keynes UK
UKOW05f1848180314

228381UK00002B/76/P